W9-BTF-551

NEW ENGLAND
On My Mind

The
Globe
Pequot
Press

GUILFORD, CONNECTICUT

Local color on Cape Ann, Massachusetts
JANE BOOTH VOLLERS

Copyright © 2003 by The Globe Pequot Press

All rights reserved. No part of this book may be reproduced or transmitted in any form by any means, electronic or mechanical, including photocopying and recording, or by any information storage and retrieval system, except as may be expressly permitted by the 1976 Copyright Act or by the publisher. Requests for permission should be made in writing to The Globe Pequot Press, P.O. Box 480, Guilford, Connecticut 06437.

Project editor: Hrissi Haldezos
Title page: Sunrise over Magalloway Mountain, New Hampshire, Alan Briere

Library of Congress Cataloging-in-Publication Data is available.
ISBN 0-7627-2514-1

Manufactured in the United States of America
First Edition/First Printing

Lush field in Redding, Connecticut JANE BOOTH VOLLERS

Though the landscape of New England presents the sharpest of contrasts, from gentle meadow and forest land to the rugged 5,000-foot peaks of the Presidential Range in New Hampshire, there is a kind of homogeneity about the whole that is a matter of spirit rather than of the land itself. If you love New England some inner sense will tell you when you are there.

—STEWART BEACH, *New England in Color*

Grazing cows below Mt. Greylock, Massachusetts A. BLAKE GARDNER

Birches and mist in New Hampshire's White Mountain National Forest WILLIAM NEILL / LARRY ULRICH STOCK

Spider web, Cedar Lake, Connecticut
JANE BOOTH VOLLERS

*My New England is both a place and a state of mind,
sometimes hard to fathom, but rarely boring: it is a
rugged symphony of rocky pastures and choppy
birch-clad hills where partridges sun and deer flaunt
white flags; it is a cold, immortal sea crashing against
a coast steeped in tradition.*

—FRANK WOOLNER, *My New England*

Fragrant *Rosa rugosa* flourishes in coastal New England.
JANE BOOTH VOLLERS

A stony soil made sailors of men who had intended to be planters, and hardly a New England village did not, in some way, feel the sea's influence.

—*The American Heritage Book of Great Historic Places*

A weathered fence near the village of Corea,
off the Gulf of Maine TERRY DONNELLY

RICHARD V. PROCOPIO

RICHARD V. PROCOPIO

A. BLAKE GARDNER

Doesn't everyone, regardless of domicile, have a little of New England in his soul?

—FRANK WOOLNER, *My New England*

DEAN ABRAMSON

JANE BOOTH VOLLERS

JANE BOOTH VOLLERS

RICHARD V. PROCOPIO

JANE BOOTH VOLLERS

DEAN ABRAMSON

At work on Plimouth Plantation, Massachusetts ALAN BRIERE

*Poor, honest, and unworldly, the Pilgrims
wanted only to live their lives in their own
particular way. Unlike most colonists, they did
not seek to expand their territory. But from
the rock at Plymouth there emanated ripples
of great importance for the history of America.*

—The American Heritage Book of Great Historic Places

Glorious afternoon on Isle au Haut, Maine RICHARD V. PROCOPIO

Closing the fence at Sturbridge Village, Massachusetts
STEPHEN TRIMBLE

Shoemaker, Sturbridge Village STEPHEN TRIMBLE

Puritanism, believing itself quick with the seed of religious liberty, laid, without knowing it, the egg of democracy.

—JAMES RUSSELL LOWELL,
New England Two Centuries Ago

The Round Barn at Hancock Shaker Village, Massachusetts JANE BOOTH VOLLERS

Hancock Shaker Village JANE BOOTH VOLLERS

Weathered barn and early fall colors near Lemington, Vermont JOHN BARGER

If you were going to be a farmer, you could hardly choose a worse place than
New England. . . . The soil is rocky, the terrain steep, and the weather so bad
that people take actual pride in it. A year in Vermont, according to the old saw,
is "nine months of winter followed by three months of very poor sledding."

—BILL BRYSON, *A Walk in the Woods*

JANE BOOTH VOLLERS

RICHARD V. PROCOPIC

Springtime in New Hampshire ALAN BRIERE

Many New England stone fences built between 1700 and 1875 were laid
by gangs of workers who piled stones at the rate of so much per rod.
Edwin Way Teale says that in the latter years of the past century, before
economic and social developments began obliterating some of the walls,
there were a hundred thousand miles of stone fences in New England.

—WILLIAM LEAST HEAT MOON, *Blue Highways*

Block Island walls, Rhode Island JANE BOOTH VOLLERS

ALAN BRIERE

JANE BOOTH VOLLERS

Strawberry picking JANE BOOTH VOLLERS

A. BLAKE GARDNER

JANE BOOTH VOLLERS

Here and there along the highways roadside produce stands brimmed with pumpkins and squash and other autumn fruits. It was like a day trip to heaven.

—BILL BRYSON,
The Lost Continent: Travels in Small-Town America

JANE BOOTH VOLLERS

Apple picking in Connecticut JANE BOOTH VOLLERS

Autumn's bounty   JANE BOOTH VOLLERS

Crane Memorial Reservation in Massachusetts A. BLAKE GARDNER

At home in Cushing, Maine JANE BOOTH VOLLERS

Peacham country store in Vermont TERRY DONNELLY

Then the sun came out and the wind came up and the bright foliage of the New Hampshire autumn shivered and began to fall. A shower of lemon and scarlet and gold washed across our windshield. In every town, people were out raking leaves and children were playing in piles of leaves.

—CHARLES KURALT, *A Life on the Road*

Raking season in Maine RICK SCHAFER

Beaver lodge in morning mist, Massachusetts A. BLAKE GARDNER

ALAN BRIERE

Canada geese in flight ALAN BRIERE

There are Virginia deer and black bear in these woods. Beaver, once almost extinct, came back with the hardwoods. The fisher—fierce member of the weasel family—roams these woods, looking for its choice food—the porcupine; and when that animal is in short supply, it turns to red squirrels, chipmunks, and grouse.

—WILLIAM O. DOUGLAS, *My Wilderness*

Northern pitcher plants drink the morning dew, Acadia National Park.
TOM BLAGDEN / LARRY ULRICH STOCK

Berry bushes and grasses amid lichen-covered granite,
Acadia National Park, Maine MARY LIZ AUSTIN

Bull moose silhouetted in sparkling lake KEN ARCHER

Fishing the St. Croix River, Maine STEPHEN TRIMBLE

A Maine fishing camp! The state that's given American culture the lumberman, the lobsterman, the Maine guide, has also given it this: the camp in the woods where the trout bite even faster than the black flies, the salmon leap into your canoe of their own volition, the griddle cakes come stuffed with blueberries, the loon calls at night, the moose bellows, and you sleep soundly under thick wool blankets even in July.

—W. D. WETHERELL, *One River More*

Aquatic rushes growing in Eagle Lake, Acadia National Park TOM BLAGDEN / LARRY ULRICH STOCK

Canadian dogwood, New Hampshire ED COOPER

Blueberries on Champlain Mountain, Acadia National Park LARRY ULRICH

JANE BOOTH VOLLERS

October is the month of painted leaves. Their rich glow now flashes around the world. As fruits and leaves and the day itself acquire a bright tint just before they fall, so the year near is setting. October is sunset sky; November the later twilight.

—HENRY DAVID THOREAU, *Autumnal Tints*

Autumnal reflections in the White Mountains TONY SWEET

Along the shoreline of Bubble Pond,
Acadia National Park MARY LIZ AUSTIN

A waiting sugar maple, New Hampshire ALAN BRIERE

Maine farmstead DEAN ABRAMSON

The Old Man of the Mountain natural rock profile,
Franconia Notch, New Hampshire ALAN BRIERE

Winter campers pulling equipment sleds, in Maine's Allagash Wilderness ALAN BRIERE

Color and snow in the White Mountains of New Hampshire

TONY SWEET

Vermont rooftops in winter TONY SWEET

JANE BOOTH VOLLERS

*Vermont farmers, back each side of the turn
of the century, loved a good blizzard.*

—MURRAY HOYT, *Vermont: A Special World*

The Old Round Church, Richmond, Vermont GEORGE WUERTHNER

Ruffled feathers JANE BOOTH VOLLERS

Sugar maple sap buckets on a Vermont farm GEORGE WUERTHNER

Tapping a sugar maple GEORGE WUERTHNER

We're tappin' trees my grandparents' parents tapped. We look at it like this: a corn farmer can eat corn from the same fields his great-grandfather planted, but he can't eat from the same stalk. But an old syrupin' family eats from the same tree.

—TOM HUNTER, quoted in *Blue Highways* by William Least Heat Moon

Egrets along the Connecticut shoreline   A. BLAKE GARDNER

There is a sumptuous variety about the New England weather that compels the stranger's admiration—and regret. The weather is always doing something there; always attending strictly to business; always getting up new designs and trying them on people to see how they will go. But it gets through more business in Spring than in any other season. In the Spring I have counted one hundred and thirty-six different kinds of weather inside of twenty-four hours.

—MARK TWAIN

Spring apple blossoms, Vermont   A. BLAKE GARDNER

Green Animals Topiary Garden, Portsmouth, Rhode Island JANE BOOTH VOLLERS

JANE BOOTH VOLLERS

Springtime in Providence, Rhode Island LAURENCE PARENT

There is something charming and delightful about Rhode Island.
Its small size gives it the winsome traits of an exquisite miniature.

—PEARL BUCK, *Pearl Buck's America*

Mill near Cape Cod Bay, Massachusetts   TOM TILL

Summer is . . . [the] shade of elms and maples in New England.

—ARCHIBALD MacLEISH, *Sweet Land of Liberty*

A good catch, Maine RICHARD V. PROCOPIO

Sunrise on the St. Croix River, Maine STEPHEN TRIMBLE

A. BLAKE GARDNER

STEPHEN TRIMBLE

A something in a summer's day,
As slow her flambeaux burn away,
Which solemnizes me.

A something in a summer's noon,—
An azure depth, a wordless tune,
Transcending ecstasy.

—EMILY DICKINSON

In the "off" and empty season, after the tides had erased all signs of a hundred thousand human feet, it was hard to believe that the beach could be owned or claimed by anyone.

—JOHN HAY, *The Great Beach*

Daybreak, Cape Cod National Seashore LAURENCE PARENT

Block Island, Rhode Island JANE BOOTH VOLLERS

Enjoying Coast Guard Beach, Eastham,
on Cape Cod JANE BOOTH VOLLERS

Racing the America's Cup, off Newport, Rhode Island JANE BOOTH VOLLERS

Hoisting the sail RICHARD V. PROCOPIO

Summer playmates, off Cape Cod JANE BOOTH VOLLERS

Eye-catcher on Philbin Beach, Martha's Vineyard RICHARD V. PROCOPIO

Catching waves on Cape Cod JANE BOOTH VOLLERS

Exchange Street, Portland DEAN ABRAMSON

Portland, Maine RICHARD V. PROCOPIO

Following pages: Tidewater rapids at low tide, Reid State Park on Maine's Georgetown Island

SCOTT T. SMITH / LARRY ULRICH STOCK

Morning light bathing Stonington Harbor, Deer Island, Maine TERRY DONNELLY

Mt. Desert Island, Maine INGER HOGSTROM

Chesuncook Village, Maine RICHARD V. PROCOPIO

Painting on Nantucket Island JANE BOOTH VOLLERS

Hammonasset Beach State Park, Connecticut
A. BLAKE GARDNER

Interior stairs of the Cape Cod Highland Light at sunset
STEPHEN TRIMBLE

Maine's West Quoddy Head Lighthouse LAURENCE PARENT

Mussel shells and seaweed at low tide, Deer Isle, Maine MARY LIZ AUSTIN

Tidepool shells on Mt. Desert Island, Maine WILLIAM NEILL / LARRY ULRICH STOCK

Fisherman's Memorial Statue, Gloucester, Massachusetts ALAN BRIERE

Pemaquid Point Lighthouse, Maine STEPHEN TRIMBLE

MARY LIZ AUSTIN

RICHARD V. PROCOPIO

In Maine, lobster is a way of life. STEPHEN TRIMBLE

Lobster house at Mackerel Cove, on Bailey's Island, Maine GEORGE WUERTHNER

On Maine's Penobscot Bay DEAN ABRAMSON

Community bulletin board, Monhegan Island, Maine STEPHEN TRIMBLE

Boston Public Garden, Massachusetts STEPHEN TRIMBLE

Acorn Street, Beacon Hill, Boston ALAN BRIERE

When they came to the corner of Beacon Street there was the police car with four policemen that Clancy had sent from headquarters. The policemen held back the traffic so Mrs. Mallard and the ducklings could march across the street, right on into the Public Garden.

—ROBERT McCLOSKEY, *Make Way for Ducklings*

Newbury Street, Boston STEPHEN TRIMBLE

The mighty looms of New England's textile industry   LAURENCE PARENT

New Englanders gave us codfish and quahogs and atomic submarines.
They gave us the America's Cup Races and Waltham watches, town
meetings and mill towns, village greens and fall colors.

—TED SMART AND DAVID GIBBON, *New England*

Beaver trapper, New Hampshire   DEAN ABRAMSON

Coloring note cards, Massachusetts   A. BLAKE GARDNER

Making taffy in Provincetown, Cape Cod   FRANK S. BALTHIS

Hikers celebrating atop Maine's Mt. Katahdin—the northern terminus of the Appalachian Trail BART SMITH

Having slumped, scrambled, rolled, bounced, and walked, by turns, over this scraggy country, I arrived upon a side-hill, or rather a side-mountain, where rocks, gray, silent, rocks, were the flocks and herds that pastured, chewing a rocky cud at sunset.

—HENRY DAVID THOREAU,
The Maine Woods

Sunset on Cadillac Mountain, Acadia National Park DEAN ABRAMSON

I sing New England, as she lights her fire
In every Prairie's midst; and where the bright
Enchanting stars shine pure through Southern night,
She still is there, the guardian on the tower,
To open for the world a purer hour.

—WILLIAM ELLERY CHANNING, *New England*

THEY MADE IT POSSIBLE

New England on My Mind would not have been possible without the creative and technical skills of the professional photographers who succeeded in a difficult task—capturing the history, natural beauty, and people of New England.

From the mountains of Vermont to the shoreline of Connecticut, New England contains a breathtaking array of beautiful images, but transforming these images onto film requires more than just a camera. It takes an eye for composition, technical expertise, patience, and the sheer determination to obtain a memorable shot rather than a mere snapshot.

The photographers who contributed to *New England on My Mind* provided this extra skill and effort. They hiked, climbed, waited, and watched to get the best possible images from all across New England.

To all the talented photographers who contributed to *New England on My Mind*, thank you.

—THE GLOBE PEQUOT PRESS

Photographers in *New England on My Mind*

Dean Abramson	Laurence Parent
Ken Archer	Richard V. Procopio
Mary Liz Austin	Rick Schafer
Frank S. Balthis	Bart Smith
John Barger	Scott T. Smith
Tom Blagden	Tony Sweet
Alan Briere	Tom Till
Ed Cooper	Stephen Trimble
Terry Donnelly	Larry Ulrich
A. Blake Gardner	Jane Booth Vollers
Inger Hogstrom	George Wuerthner
William Neill	

And the photo agency:
Larry Ulrich Stock Photography, Inc.

SOURCE ACKNOWLEDGMENTS

The publisher gratefully acknowledges the following sources:

page 3, Stewart Beach, *New England in Color* (New York: Hastings House, Publishers, Inc., 1969).

page 7, Frank Woolner, *My New England* (Stone Wall Press, 1972).

page 8, *The American Heritage Book of Great Historic Places* (New York: American Heritage Publishing, 1957).

page 10, Woolner, *My New England*.

page 12, *The American Heritage Book of Great Historic Places*.

page 14, James Russell Lowell, *New England Two Centuries Ago* from John Bartlett, *Familiar Quotations* (Boston: Little, Brown, 1919), No. 7369.

page 16, Bill Bryson, *A Walk in the Woods* (New York: Broadway Books, 1998).

page 18, William Least Heat Moon, *Blue Highways* (New York: Little, Brown & Company, 1982).

page 21, Bill Bryson, *The Lost Continent: Travels in Small-Town America* (New York: Harper & Row, 1989).

page 26, Charles Kuralt, *A Life on the Road* (New York: G.P. Putnam's Sons, 1990).

page 29, William O. Douglas, *My Wilderness* (New York: Doubleday, 1960) as quoted in *The Mountain Reader* (Guilford, Conn.: The Lyons Press, 2000).

page 33, W. D. Wetherell, *One River More* (Guilford, Conn.: The Lyons Press, 1998).

page 38, Henry David Thoreau, "Autumnal Tints" reprinted in *Henry David Thoreau: Collected Essays and Poems* (New York: The Library of America, 2001).

page 47, Murray Hoyt, *Vermont: A Special World* (Montpelier, Vt.: *Vermont Life* Magazine, 1969).

page 51, quoted in William Least Heat Moon, *Blue Highways*.

page 53, Mark Twain, as quoted from a speech at dinner of New England Society; New York, 22 December 1876.

page 55, Pearl S. Buck, *Pearl Buck's America* (Bartholomew House, Ltd., 1971).

page 56, Archibald MacLeish, "Sweet Land of Liberty," quoted in *Collier's*, 8 July 1955.

page 59, *The Complete Poems of Emily Dickinson* (New York: Little, Brown & Company, 1924).

page 60, John Hay, "Who Owns the Beach?" (1986) from *The Great Beach* (University of New England Press, 1997) as quoted in *The Seacoast Reader* (Guilford, Conn.: The Lyons Press, 1999).

page 89, Robert McCloskey, *Make Way for Ducklings* (New York: The Viking Press, 1941, 1969).

page 91, Ted Smart and David Gibbon, *New England* (New York: Mayflower Books Inc., 1980), first published by Colour Library International, Inc., New York.

page 93, Henry David Thoreau, *The Maine Woods* as quoted in *The Mountain Reader* (Guilford, Conn.: The Lyons Press, 2000).

page 94, William Ellery Channing, *New England* from John Bartlett, *Familiar Quotations* (Boston: Little, Brown, 1919), No. 7232.

KEN ARCHER